The
Length
of
an
Afternoon

D1736169

The Length of an Afternoon

Poems

James Cushing

cahuenga
PRESS

Acknowledgments

Grateful acknowledgement is made to the following magazines where some of these poems, some in different form, first appeared: *Artful Dodge; Asylum Annual; Chants; Confluence; Cyanosis; Kansas Quarterly; Lullwater Review; Madison Review; Negative Capability; Oxford; Paper Salad; Pearl; Sycamore Review.*

"Ambiguous Message," "No Blame," "After Eight Years" and "Pantomime" were the winning poems in the 1995 "Warlords of the Subculture" poetry contest sponsored by *Renegade* magazine.

Personal thanks:

In Los Angeles: my fellow-members of Cahuenga Press, Laurel Ann Bogen, Wanda Coleman, Dennis Cooper, Bob Flanagan (1951-1994), Michael C. Ford, Amy Gerstler, Charlene Knowlton, Harvey Kubernick, Bill Mohr, Robert Peters, Joan Jobe Smith, Jean Stearns, David St. John, and everyone at Beyond Baroque.

In San Luis Obispo: Greg Boyd, Nicholas Campbell, Joan Campbell, Kevin Clark, Sauny Dills, David Frank, Marian Galczenski, Linda Halisky, Michael Hannon, Mary Kay Harrington, Larry Inchausti, David Kann, Karl Kempton, Susan Marsala, Steven Marx, Paul Miklowitz, Dian Souza, Marian Stevens, Kevin Patrick Sullivan.

In Salt Lake City: Donald Revell, Claudia Keelan

In New York: Jonathon Robinson-Apell, David Trinidad

In London: Donald Martin Smith

Book and cover design by Greg Boyd
Cover painting by Glen Starkey
Printed by McNaughton & Gunn, Inc., Saline, MI

Cahuenga Press is owned, financed and operated by its poet-members James Cushing, Phoebe MacAdams, Harry E. Northup, Holly Prado Northup, and Cecilia Woloch. Our common goal is to create fine books of poetry by poets whose work we admire and respect; to make poetry actual in the world in ways which honor both individual creative freedom and cooperative support.

Cahuenga Press
1256 N. Mariposa
Los Angeles, CA 90029

To my daughter Iris

Contents

Our Love is Here to Stay / 11
Lime Kiln Creek / 13
Come Day, Go Day / 14
The Constant Lamp / 15
Pantomime / 16
Lovers in a Landscape / 17
Systematic Romanticism / 18
Histories of Great Men and Women / 20
Little Mortal / 21
The Cave of Making / 22
The Father at Rest / 25
Consolation / 27
Asleep Against the Breasts of a Friend (after Sappho) / 29
Letter to a Painter (1) / 31
Letter to a Painter (2) / 32
Twins / 33
There's No Telling / 34
Vacant Places / 35
After Eight Years / 38
Ambiguous Message / 39
Twenty-First Century Art / 41
Assembling the Sea / 43
No Blame / 44
Albert Ayler / 46
Wind Tunnel / 47
The True and Secret Reason / 48
Legends of the Marketplace / 49
Wavering Phantom / 50
In Distant Trees / 51
Comical Conversations / 52
Good Neighbors / 53

Personal Problems / 55
End of May / 57
The Riverman / 58
The Good Curve of the Year / 59
The Puzzle of the Reward / 61
A Bramble / 62
The New Year / 64
Foolish Paradise / 65
The Lord's Subject / 68
A Piece of Blood / 72
The Kingdom of Ends / 74
Swimming Back to Land / 75
Well May the World Go (When I'm Far Away) / 76
The Length of an Afternoon / 77

President Clinton floats through my bloodstream on Air Force One with his magnetic wife and mysterious daughter.

On his lap is a classified document called *The Book of Five Dreams*.

In the first dream, he's a robin with a chest the size of a three-bedroom apartment, chirping in the morning sun.

In the second dream, he's a leopard howling in a circle of donkeys and elephants.

In the third and fourth dreams, he doesn't really do anything but sit at a banquet table watching my ex-wife foxtrot with my father.

In the fifth and last dream he climbs down into the earth like a miner and gets transformed into ore—a solid mass melting down into a wallet-sized hunk.

I awake sleepy, vaguely deaf, unable to answer simple questions.

Indeed, what forces us at all to suppose that there is an essential opposition of "true" and "false"? Is it not sufficient to assume degrees of apparentness and, as it were, lighter and darker shadows and shades of appearance—different "values," to use the language of painters? Why couldn't the world that concerns us—be a fiction? And if somebody asked, "but to a fiction there surely belongs an author?" —couldn't one answer simply: why? Doesn't this "belongs" belong to the fiction, too?

Nietzsche, *Beyond Good and Evil*, sec. 34

The
Length
of
an
Afternoon

Our Love is Here to Stay

(for Marian Stevens)

The nakedness of women is a mighty work,
"a portion of eternity too great for the eye of man" (Blake)
and I, a man in this presence, stand among the life
drawing students and yearn, not knowing for what.

The two nude women pose a form of love and waiting,
its contours and its planes. I sense myself as living
on the black side of a bedroom mirror. The models
look in a direction that includes me, a vase
of flowers, some words in crayon on a wall
near where I hang, framed. Their waiting
takes a shape of letters in a word
of which these women could be made,
invokes the calm of having landed after wandering
through the ether of cities, alone.

I take a bite of my pound cake. Clothed women
behind easels rub planes with turpenoid-darkened
paper towels, looking at color so intently I can tell
what size they feel they are, what forms of love
and waiting each woman knows. For some, drawing
embraces, for some it windows the world,
for some it allows a freedom that includes aggression,
envy, the flex of female muscle under sunlight.
The pose is not a prayer for mercy or forgiveness,
not an image of innocence or sex; the models have
no use for these. What we feel is, *C'est moi,*
not the illusion of it, nor the wish for it to be true
as the cake in my mouth is true. What amazes us

11

is the truth of feeling no gap, of seeing ourselves
as a pair of naked women, self and self,
light and light, substance and substance. I sit heavily,
my doubled fear and courage made beautiful
as food in a ritual, eaten by eyes and hands.
I feel within me a great bird, rising from a plain
beneath the moon. These women are her wings.

Why should anyone need pictures or poems anyway,
I can hear the bird asking. Here is our answer:
our losses demand them. Exhausted by time
and its disasters, having squeezed each word we know
out of our favorite old pens, flattened by the heavy length
of our darkening afternoon, we pause and wait,
and then we start to love. We begin our loving by leaping,
leaping off a tall building, knowing we won't be hurt
as long as we know we won't be hurt,
yet we have been hurting since our birth, but only now
can we embrace its goodness, its work of filling
our waiting with loving, blessing our loving with waiting.
I am seeing myself in these two women
and the poem is how I am doing it. The shadow on this page
is the way light does it. And we marvel that such plans
could have been dreamed for us this cold and windy day,
we who have never seen ourselves lit up this way,
but here we are now, in this light which is pure metaphor
for only its own private life, which is us.
For this we have waited, in this joy we wait.
Wrap them in sapphire voices, sing "Ave Maria."
Two nude women, posed before a class
of women drawing them, amen.

Lime Kiln Creek

When we agreed to start working on autumn
the last days of August felt softer, more obliging.
Butterflies made no plans all season,
refused to tell what they expected us to make.
We couldn't invent anything out of their doodles
and familiarities. The scent of old gardenias
shaped the evening's receptive air into one
adult motion toward God. I told myself
I could be warmer as I eavesdropped on my daughter
singing "dark, dark, dark" in her tent.
My wife turned to me in our tent. The campfire
popped and fell silent.

That's the real story of adult conversation, the fear
of being reduced to the body and its echoes
of every other body, the ways we stand weakened,
neither speaking nor moving in front of our desire
for all we don't and can't know about each other
despite the nakedness of gesture, breath, placement
on this fragile, careless earth. The groups of men
and women, larger children transformed into grown-ups
by our temporary gaze, look willful as ultramarine stripes
beneath fire-alarm red. We want to believe
they're telling one another nothing but the truth
about their lives. We have to rise and dress.
I must tell you what has happened.

Come Day, Go Day

I'm compelled to tell the world about our love
the way compulsive shoppers pull toward sales of bottles,
magnets, pulleys, Beatles picture sleeves.
I don't trust my eyes in your presence.
The bedroom and what we said in it may never be subject to
national attention. Your arm turns there, and I must have it.
Your signature shows slight changes in the light
when September deepens into browns and reds, and
desks awaken into femininity. God Himself shows up in
shadows of gestures we make at those desks, those impossible
notebooks filling up with our cloudy, echoplexed words of love.

I'm a violin in that bedroom, where red is calm, where fear
never stalks, where no beast stares down any dark fires. Here we need
no wishful resumes. Once we needed water; now a drowned man's voice
resumes its lullaby of names and places. Now we form a hunter
together, thinking only later of a missing pain, a tiny cancer
growing in the dream's lame mansion. We still choke up
when we consider how margins can be placed anywhere,
how history remains the easiest part of the dream to read.

The Constant Lamp

The skeleton: is this made of water, too?
Photographs we intended to take of one another,
geraniums in pots on distant balconies: are these
made of water, too? Certainly the barman calling "two minutes"
to his slow-moving customers is made of water
but if the soundtrack to their exits turns plush and confessional
the dazzling welter of our experience dims, and sexual hope
cascades, the cooling droplets strangely hard, oppressed.
Summer, whiting out into autumn, refuses to lift its pencil
from our calendar of heroes, its plot
involving prizes in the center
of the body. Wherever you are, your hand
gets ridden by a fallen tree.

Equally important is the space between the lovers
in these photographs. Clearly
all they want to do is sleep, even
sitting at a table with flowers and candles is too much effort
for them: the black fluid in their bones is about to
flow out, engulf their arms and eyes, and quiet them.
Travel remains unknown to them. I can't even
see them; they're blocked by a woman who by pure chance
has my last name. She moves to the left.
By then they have vanished like summer
with its foolishness on broad backs of mosquitos
who return to pines I enter again like a part of a stream.
Amazingly, it is still wet, still flowing across its inch.

Pantomime

On All Saints' Day, the lovers remove their human being costumes;
their wings, ragged from folding, please the air with curves.
The dark-haired man, dressed in red, smiles at the thought of one secret;
the blonde, dressed in tight black, whispers "What are you thinking?"
In less than half an hour, this scene, too, will have vanished;
nothing, not even her whisper, will be left behind.
Yet our time seemed to turn and fall so slowly, so densely;
each evening loomed like a greasy mountain we had to climb
with heavy packs. What made inventing wings difficult was seeing
two weeks into the future, which we did regularly with
vast and complex accuracy. The past, now there
we had problems: one morning one closet pole
snapped under our laughable garments.
Next morning, Mozart rang from dawn
to noon, like a low angel unhindered by our tries
at flight. Tonight, your father and my mother
ask if they may have this dance;
underneath them, we sit peeling oranges, licking
our fingers, quizzing one another on the
many names of love. Weary of our winglessness,
we strap on our strange new bodies,
squeeze our house keys' teeth for luck,
go hunting for reasons to peep under curtains,
to answer the RSVP the full moon left on the sill.

Apparently, no bird or bush intends to tell this story.
Feeling faint with hunger, eyes red
with allergies and love, we hear a second voice
in which our faces turn as pumpkin-colored as the sky,
the grass, the distant hills, the ocean. "Just enough
to sustain life," she sings. And that is all.

16

Lovers in a Landscape

Disguised as a mountain and an ocean,
they stirred from their state-owned bed.
Kites made of honey, red peppers and pistachios
failed to carry them across one field.

Can you see an alphabet of flags
On the rim, spelling their names four times?
Those four poles holding up the sky cannot
be named, though they are plainly visible,

though we know they glimpsed them during
the woman's dream of ghosts hauling mirrors
across their bedroom. A month
or less later, clumped in their bed,

they recall how it felt to learn the language. His animal hair,
that's what she's thinking. Meeting my maker,
that's what she's thinking. No distance lies
between us now, that's what she's thinking, and

her left half of their rained-on sky is a work in progress
called "Our Life," too big to see at once.
Their comforter, pulled through the bruise of night,
feels harder than wisdom, sharper-cornered.

They forgot the most important thing.
The next-to-last section of their comforter
hauls itself across a long, dusty stage
but latecomers always get front row seats.

Systematic Romanticism

Herr Zauberberg, take heed;
what would be simpler than spreading our black wings?
We fell for hours through this block-printed chimney, wearing
our green felt hats. We landed at old, beloved
problems we kept solving on our feet,
no longer new, no longer apple-shaped.
We forgot to put on our heads today.
Don't tell me about your pattern baldness,
ancient academic failures. Our new way of living
shines, glares, becomes unwatchable.
We guard remaining daylight like a Chopin autograph.

Surprise, as always, is issue number one
for men picking at their hands in gymnasiums
as everyone applauds a visiting fireman's talk about home
alarms. As close to himself as fingers to fingers,
he pushes against a sticky cloud
of bills coated with dreams, ocean bottom rocks
their preferred symbol. His week comes interpreted;
a photo painted over means this man has tried to swim it.
In bed before midnight with his wife, he has to ask her why
their puppy seems more somber in the summer,
why squirrels favor smoky back yards.

I think you see why cars are rightful metaphor for them
although she tells him she prefers
an abacus involved in the center of a diamond,
braces of flags, hexagrams, airport sign,
emblems on a dance floor swaying
to Miracles and Stones.

The hills they love recede into curtains of lavender.
Bubbles start to inflate;
many already float across the ceiling fan blades.
Present even when they hide,
one-inch strips of cochineal question us.

Histories of Great Men and Women

Our work? It's only what we do.
The month ends in fuzzy yellow phone calls anyway.

Ghosts invite us into bed with their lovers,
then prevent us from wanting their humid curves.
Nostalgia perfumes the caves we wake up in.
Part of the game is we don't know we've awakened
yet we feel something missing from the pleasures
Tuesday evenings on waterfronts provide.
Mists and oils once added up to meals.
Mittens for hands, plates for faces, squiggles for hair
gave us most of what we needed. With transparent orchestras
we had it made, balanced between
the awkward and the simple, like a salad.

Oh vegetable-motif calendars, September days
clotting with compulsions to dance and buy furniture,
you're what my body copies when I move!
I read all about you but the article didn't mention
you walking away from me toward the house we bought.
What's impressive about the house is our faces in it:
sharp, clean-lined, like darts. We're certain to be tossed,
like them, with our conclusions about the meanings
of clouds behind the trees, why we find
warm meteor-showered nights depressing,
why moons keep damaging our autumn.

The dream, inhibited from clarity, hides its kisses under its quilt
and sings important, secret songs. Scraps of them swirl
in eddies all day. This is our work. One magnolia.

Little Mortal

I love men's names only for their sound, you said,
having disengaged your hooks, unsnapped your snaps.

What sound ruined the opening of your flower?
You whistled along its surfaces as evenings
spoke to you in Spanish, started to interpret
the sound your secrets shied from,
creases in music where you could sit and
hear your dense yet unencumbered flower.
Now I start misinterpreting your field
because your flower—no, this portion—
shows me a face in which I am an infant,
rolling, rolling, about to drop off the slanted earth,
and no man or woman may catch me
or watch my rolling fall.

Then you started telling me details from your dream
in which I sat scrunched-up on your floor. Surrounding
gardens smelled of soap, fennel, John F. Kennedy roses.
Good thing we taped it, huh? It'll be out later this year:
When Logics Die, on Sisyphus, distributed by Epic.
Nothing in the racks duplicates its persuasive coherence
produced by seeing through available forms to the atoms
motoring them. I called the producer a minute ago
and learned I had no room in its mansion. You have a place
in its west wing, like a blackbird has its place in a hot blue sky
the color of your Reagan-era jeans.

The Cave of Making

1.

Here silence is turned into objects more private than a bedroom
but without a bedroom's secret: it is evident what must go on.
All is subordinate here to a function, to sharpen hearing:
we're not musicians but we know our mystery from the inside.

Without a bedroom's secret, it is evident what must go on
between us, near the piled-up clothes beneath the window.
We're not musicians but we know our mystery from the inside
out; we have scraped our past of its rind and grated it.

Between us, near the piled-up clothes beneath the window,
two squares of light mark out a type of map to the path that leads
out. We have scraped our past of its rind and grated it
for a melted sandwich, the sort we love to eat in bed.

Two squares of light mark out a type of map to the path that leads
up to where we lived before we met. I know I'd trade those dwellings
for a melted sandwich, the sort we love to eat in bed
together, after the movie and the questions it raised in us.

Up to where we lived before we met, I know I'd trade those dwellings
even if it meant we had to relive it all from 22 to now
together, after the movies and the questions it raised in us
got forgotten in the grids and spirals of the immanent equinox.

Even if it meant we had to relive it all from 22 to now,
right down to the flat tires and lumpy old beanbag chairs that
got forgotten in the grids and spirals of the immanent equinox,
I would stand in line, I would sign my name along with yours

right down to the flat tires and lumpy old beanbag chairs that
implicate themselves in our signatures. And then the fires?
I would stand in line, I would sign my name along with yours
on that document of fire. Later the embers would learn our words,

implicate themselves in our signatures, and then the fires
they remembered would shudder open. Morning pours ice
on that document of fire later. The embers would learn our words
if we could trust them with that awful information

they remembered would shudder open. Morning pours ice;
here silence is turned into objects more private than a bedroom,
if we could trust them. With that awful information,
all is subordinate here to a function, to sharpen hearing.

2.

I wish I could show you the function: from your perspective you'd notice
unknowable nomads, lip-smacking lamps of bark and honey.
Both of us became self-conscious at a moment of numinous trust.
We knew, subjectively, that all was possible. What else was there to do but talk?

Unknowable nomads, lip-smacking lamps of bark and honey,
the endless fog of the twelfth century somehow present in the twentieth:
we knew, subjectively, that all was possible. What else was there to do but talk
until we had exhausted our interest in those possibilities of stasis and change?

The endless fog of the twelfth century, somehow present in the twentieth,
takes ever-more alarming forms as it settles in around the marketplace.
Until we had exhausted our interest in those possibilities of stasis and change
this culture made no place for either one of us. That little problem

takes ever-more alarming forms as it settles in around the marketplace.
I remember when we started getting used to the idea, finally accepting that
this culture made no place for either one of us. That little problem,
our future, got flattened out into a path we still walk on.

I remember when we started getting used to the idea, finally accepting that
I wish I could show you the function. From your perspective, you'd notice
our future got flattened out into a path we still walk on.
Both of us became self-conscious at a moment of numinous trust.

The Father at Rest

Autumn, a quiet matter of
refrigeration and flying horses,
tells me what to ask my father in
my dream.   He is hovering around me,
the man whose heavy shoes and hat
I tried twelve years to learn to read,
whose photograph shines in my bedroom black
as the stone on the tomb of the unknown soldier,
whose voice returns with the force of six whispers.
Another day flags in awful wind over shaking lemon trees,
rises like bread through ovens the color of winter.
Where beasts stand waiting in wordless yards
my father sits, wearing his mask.
His body is a scribble on a beach,
a blurry panel of muscle and sound.
Yes, this is our body, he tells me,
counting aloud the pages in his hand.
Moving maroon and silver planes around,
he keeps my mother inside their tiny house
in one black room where they awaken
from nightly dreams of iron gardens.
Some of the things that make him happy include
my reluctance to see him move
his body, excruciatingly slow,
completely convincing when walking
over wooden tunnels of ancient Greek sunlight
as the equinox twitches a pail of rain.

I know he likes to force things till they break:
awnings, tomatoes, prawns the size of cats.
"Compress that meat," he likes to say.

Before he speaks, the herons dip for fish.
He never asks about the rules against touching.
What matters is neither lack of purpose nor
the hurried pace of the weave.
I am an unbuilt frame, a mutterer,
the one in the white plastic bottle
always turning past the stone gate,
the stone age, the stone birth, the stone
imprinted with the first butterfly,
the wisdom of our hands on one another.

Consolation

Most impressive after one a.m., the church
conceals a bearded, lilac-scented garden
behind which dreams, oblivious
to shame, light fires under tiny hats of incense.

When we say our prayers to the body of fallen sticks
and rustlings of bugs in the stack of sticks
several things occur at once:

our mouths, so busy up until a moment before,
grow slack, and our voices, no longer streams
of appreciation, dwindle.

We stand among the flames we're safe from.
We still love being held, if only by our clothes,
although "scary" is a synonym for "good."

Cars roll all night, district to district, full of men thinking of women,
then rust all day in fields with chicken bones and software.
Liars pull impossible overalls and driving gloves from graves.

Twenty dollars turns to fifty cents in ten seconds.
The monkey in my checking account groans under my butt and dies broke.
My limbs roll off my body into a field somewhere.

And all these little cuts on the backs of my hands...

And there, along the edge of the shore,
are jigsaw-puzzle pieces we dropped in 1983.

Scribbled love notes listen to birds and imitate them.

Suddenly I recall where you and I lost our ability
to distinguish one another from finches in nests.

The higher the finches appear to fly, their unclean wings
stapled to the bed, the more you see my point of view
on pity: even rain, old as the pair of shoes I found
left behind in a motel room, is a scheme of things.

I'm sure about the waves of pianos rising up out of the sea.
Now, I'm seeing your mountain when I close my eyes
over coffee. Thank you for your beautiful mountain.

It's legible if you turn it upside down.
Why did you say it was a box of chocolate crayons?

Asleep Against the Breasts of a Friend

(after Sappho)

Why, after so long, should I dream
of the early nineteen-seventies?

You were to me then a bold young woman
who sometimes closed her eyes
all night.

Crows, blackbirds
orbiting earth
knew as we knew.

Women wove crowns of leaves,
sent beautiful complaints
through white curtains,
summer afternoons.

And I yearned
and I hunted
through room after room,
stumbling against
the lingering dark,
asking.

Swallow, swallow, daughter
of wind and sky,
why me?

Why so many new arrivals?
I pack a day with them,
stretch that day into a string,
tie up the moon with it!

Waiting for my lover,
I hear a bee asking
Where is my flower?
Have you begun to forget me
or do you love some other?

I don't know which way I'm running.
My mind is part this way, part that.
I am willing but weaker than water,
and night's black sleep tangles upon my eyes.

Letter to a Painter (1)

The one recurring image in your most recent show
rises like a Chinese scrim behind a field of bones.
The ripping of a paper doll precedes
a singing woman with a camera.
At ease in her smoldering clothing, speaking
through cheesecloth, she says
those bones represent your secret.

The label under her photo of you reads "gleaner,"
which adds flavor and life to your portrait,
gives it that shimmer people stay up late to see.

Later, she filmed you climbing up
a broken staircase, stepping over
corpses of tapirs and opossums.
Why did they keep moving?

An attractive man leaned against your doorbell that night.
Romantically involved with a female impersonator, he wanted
to use your guestroom for a night of forbidden sex. Where
would you locate your work in his tradition? Who are
your ultimate progenitors?

Letter to a Painter (2)

Life these days is sweet and full, and I'm worn out at the end of them.
Too full of food to speak, the summer lies before me on its blanket,
unfolding scrap paper, looking for names.

Your last letter really clued me in
how you were using the wolf as a letter in a new alphabet.
Other recurring images accented words or punctuated groups of them.
Order entered in muffled rushes of passion and frying hair.

They failed, and their glamorous comet-trails
unite men still : "You saw them? You were there?" Power
among men is proximity to glow, its frantic, silent seconds, the heaps
of ashes after. Memory of this proximity. Access to means of articulating
this memory. Fear of failure, poor memory, unworthiness.
Propitiation. Burnt offerings. Rituals. Chants, spells,
Incantations. Cantor, shaman, priest. The voice. What is written
to be spoken. Authority giving voice to word. Interpretation. Performance
giving word to voice. Asking voice for forgiveness with voice. Silence.
Forcing voice. Concentration of energy. Editing silence out of voice.
Condensing voice. Authority over voice. History. The record of memory,
the purest dream-work. Image birthing image as book begets book.

The comet-tail image may be the best of those left to us.
The endless gesture of falling, so beautiful it hurts: there,
in one image, all of man's plight, all our hunger, our wildness.
Not as if nobody saw it coming. At thirteen, one hears a buzz from
the household piano during a lesson. No more lessons. We know what
happens then: amazing magazines, flabbergasting vegetables,
translations of buzz. An alternative alphabet. Horizons
constructed of black and coral jewels.

Twins

They scurried over the flowers.
The act of seeing is animal (walking, running,
sitting still). Their scurrying eyes loped up green stems,
probed each blossom like thieves. Born 1954, they planned
their lives in 1966, but modern society is intensely
secular, so they wasted 1979 in distant cities,
sailors over traintracks, breathing like birds.

They scurried cluelessly over the flowers
driven by the magnetism flowers
use to catch the eyes of witnesses.
Midgets stir among massive wooden blocks
fitted together into shapes of their house.
Here they could grow lifesized,
hobbled by pianos, hands shiny as playing cards.
Clarinets pinpoint their quarter-notes of knowing.
To be lifesized! To have stolen heaven!
What drumrolls and fanfares, what a night!

I know nothing of the paper or the pen.
I know the home phone of scurriers, their sticky voices adhering
like petal dust to my fingers. I know what hours they keep.
Night after night, they hang exhausted suitcoats on a stamen.
I know the imperfections in their gaits. Columns of water, oddly shaped,
fall and keep falling through summer clouds, keeping pace
with the clock. This is information in its cleanest form. But so few want
to listen to supplicants.

There's No Telling

At first, waking ourselves from August,
we told only lies about potted plants
and where their soil was from:
a little last connection with the fifties.

Later, the spirit of James Brown passed
his palm over our troubled brows.

The simplest recording of what takes place
stands with a trumpet, telling funny truths
that vanish like mild earthquakes
among well-announced sections of wind:
part blood, part pepper, part clock.

We work, and curl up in our rewards
like so much else of summer,
finding places, putting fingers there.

Thousands of pounds of love limbo beneath
arches, holding pieces of a long-forgotten blanket.
Ghosts, we call them. And always a Brazilian cloud
landing plunk on the square as summer passed
through shapes and shapes. And then a pause.

You're my fondest interruption, a catalogue
with page after page of privileged lakes
but never a model, never a turbulent pool.

We tremble as we drive from our rewards.
There's no need for them now.
Wait, it'll come to me: Bending out of the century
like soggy flowers out of a vase. Is that all right?

Vacant Places

Sunday night prepares its funeral

Out where alfalfa shines under moons fatter and lusher than ours, dry and hungry crows, champion crushers of beetles and crickets, worry at a scrap of bone, a nub of brain. Stripes of music hurry across grain and sky, boiling. Each phrase flips, enlightened by night, innocent of rain, crunching its pippin.

The middle of August   a bucket with a pinhole, imperceptibly draining

Summer had meant breakage, green humidity, hard exposed roots polished by bare feet, fear of nightmares, ballpoint initials behind strange beds, the glow of a Coleman around a hard ghost story. Everything vanishing.

Familiarity   number in all things

Only three months had passed since they moved in together, and it already seemed nothing could be done about their mood swings, their poor and clumsy choices. Every afternoon by four, they had turned into vastly different people. He sensed that he was at last pulling himself up from the muck of his childhood, sore and shoeless but in one piece. She wasn't so sure. Getting no duller with age, her velocity of mind was calming. She was still primarily sensual, but more abstracted about it. He had to reexamine the whole sexual dimension. Despite his foolish assumptions, the fundamental problem in their relationship still hadn't been solved.

A week later, he received her reply:

raspberry sherbet nail polish
and a question under
doublemint: my "hello"

the governor's office:
Elvis movies spooling
onto floors dusty with law

a meal eaten with bachelors
so long ago: now, my
husband, where are you?

another summer ends:
a net bag of beach toys
sandy on the porch at dusk

John, your phone call
composed my weekend:
nasturtiums by the door

all men handsome,
all women beautiful:
fog on the empty bay

chocolate covered
espresso beans, pink frappe
lipstick: time to go home

with one match
the room points at
books I needed then

last or first hour?
smoke, rain, a lamp in
a corner: no words

That was the whole text of her letter, no salutation, signature, return address. The stamp a standard-issue flag, right side up. The plainest possible white business envelope. He could not begin to grasp her intentions. He already knew she wrote poetry, lived somewhere near Denver (the postmark), had great expertise in vanishing. Where was she during the recent riots? Did she deal with her landlord on a first-name-only basis ("just Lynn")? What about the rumors of a birth?

After Eight Years

Now that we've forgotten our yearning
our food takes so much longer to digest.
The problem is not our fear of death, nor
who wins the right to count months by
measuring inches of the cactus. Poorer now
than ever, we want to walk around the stage
and feel the piano. Elvis Presley is still king.
You're still queen and chief ambassador. Just
when twilight starts pumping itself up in its
rubber armchair, about to tell us to drink water only,
you show up in my bed with your crunchy bell pepper,
your mystery novel, your haze. At some point during
the evening, we speak. Our talk evolves out of
changes in seasons, changes in densities of light
about which we have almost too much to say: for example,
that we miss them already. Above the dust-free earth,
assessments are submitted: it is all a wall of bricks and wind.
Pyramus and Thisbe are glimpsed undressed,
talking all night through a hole in the wall.
The muscles of her back are beautiful! Even her hands,
held so closely to the wall, invite our touch.
She knows him as one foreigner knows another.
They carry water and lanterns to an appointed place.

Ambiguous Message

In terms of blindness, deafness, dumbness
our little squiggles don't exist. Those terms
keep sitting there outside the ring of fire,
telling no stories, finding no keys. My love,
we may take any posture toward them we wish:
barometric undercurrents, endless
disputations, fear of full moons. Citizens form armies, orchestras,
sororities, communes, homeowners' associations. On our map,
they take forms of roses and geraniums
staring all night at the living room clock.

Sixty foot tall flowers might have blossomed. Look what happened instead.
What hope we had for those flowers. How wrong of us
to have had it. They blossom nonetheless, waiting at our feet like tiny
ideas. We're skittering above city blocks on a carpet,
gripping cold edges, smog in our eyes.
I am a burned and looted city, drifting in and out of sleep.
Magnetic trash accumulates. Each step
echoes, weighs more than it should
as stories in the press change shape from fruit to bone.

We are magnetic fishermen.
Is it our doing there are no fish?

But you are sleeping. In your dream your
president appears on concert stages
singing simple notes as autumn drains colors
out of nearly everything. We know why it
needs to happen. Don't worry about the light.

There are many lacunæ in our studies,
agreement is only fair. Obviously our methods
cannot be foolproof, they assume normal
responses from readers massed in lobbies,
worrying their cuticles, sipping pop, ashamed of
walking naked up to you,
putting a hand on your arm,
looking directly at you.

Twenty-First Century Art

It is convincing.
It forms a "we" where was none,
studies itself through us, and deeply.
Its meaning polaroids into what we waited for.

It shows respect for the past by betraying it.
It forgives Mozart for being there first,
forgives Beckett for closing the door.

It will not shake.
It wears details like functional clothing,
remains polite to its daughters and sons.

Its cheating heart forms one invisible vertical.
It eats all it finds on its plate, then the plate,
the table, the chairs.

It likes best the image of a scroll
unwinding, one line per hour,
twenty-four lines per page, bound
in cloth from old worn shirts, stacked
somewhere inside our chests.

In three days we make love for the first time.
It stands outside in the dark heaving earth.
Smoke relaxes all along the length of the street,
touches pavement lit by soft blue
candles. Thin autumns roll away
from us like coins.
The moon agrees with us,
bites down.

Fragrant blue zeroes
turn to us upset:
we cannot comfort fragrant blue zeroes.

It fumbles out of its clothes
toward a conclusion
(what sex is it?), strewing them
behind the tallest building,
the one that just moved
several paces to the left.
Look! She's a woman, nude
like last year, the year before.

The ease with which she shuts her eyes.

Assembling the Sea

I start with distant fields of pink geraniums,
words I forgot to write down when they counted.
I add a school of painters erasing marks, waiting
like ships in bottles for signs of land.

I bought twenty-two bottled ships.
I wanted each bottle to shine!
I will fill space like a bottled ship, that quietly,
and when comes my time to be lifted and emptied,
how high, how gladly will I raise my arms!

In the storage shed behind my garden, summer ends.
A dailiness clings to twists of pink geraniums,
binds wounds. Harvesting with brooms and scythes,
I stare at my garden astonished,
a scarecrow!
            All this foolishness
like mirrors thrust under buses
can never die I said
for I am one of the great undead
between books of poems and books of murders
I am forgetting the accent I spoke with once
upon first learning to talk foolishness

I held up my arms all day and am stronger for it
my beautiful genitals disperse into cloud-colored air
beneath a speaking pool
of geraniums artfully arranged in a word

and as September becomes October I see an elder
collecting straw that he may make his brick

No Blame

Darling, my letter to your body grows hefty.
I cannot say enough about the peaches in your warmth,
about your dark German of lunging and waking.
When I was ten, in my mother's kitchen,

staring at a linoleum compass worked into the floor,
I read each arrow as a signal: go north, go east, go fast.
The pleats of her skirt, later seasons,
quilted maps... Why carp on them?

What is "carping"? Is it a form of trouting?
I said I was ten and in my mother's kitchen.
I'm only cataloguing pieces of news
I'm not surprised look strange on top,

familiar below. My darling faces west, propped-up,
beautifully bored, paler than wind hidden trees.
Clouds of china patterns recede following trawlers,
wet matches, spent matches, dissolving wedding dresses.

Well, officer, the last thing I remember
is loving her wedding dress.... My darling is a carp.
To love her well, recall how elaborate the bones,
as many as you need, as high as you can count.

And now who remembers the story of the bones?
I was poured warm onto surfaces of bones—
couldn't use my legs for years. Resultant loneliness
gleamed inauthentically in leaky fish stores

where my featureless face hung like a moonlit kimono.
My name means "Slavish Devotion to Protocol."
I'm an open secret, filling little cells. I'm Kafka
with long hair and two pearl strands, weighing odds,

deciding whether to follow you home, my darling.

Albert Ayler

At first it seems that air itself is shaping what it sings.
        Then you hear a little boy with his bindle stick
Leaving geometry behind in burst of ash
        and tar and dust, a runaway, his body
Born many times, wearier each time the slap pries open
        the skylight, letting in rain.
Europe helped as long as she could
        but late one afternoon her Bible stopped and faded.
"Run, run!" goes the voice speaking from this music,
        and from the couch you keep telling me
"That's all right, darling, nothing's really changed between us"
        and suddenly I can't even move!

Anyway, where does music really take place? In our memories
        of each other laid end to end like bricks?
Yesterday the "run" voice became food and hurt
        the way eating often does, but
Laughing at this pain is a sign of mental health.
        Don't worry,
Everybody's confused. This love I've got
        to give away before it tears me up
Resembles a choir nudging my conscience
        like a door opening, knocking over a cup.

Wind Tunnel

Bigger than the night, and darker,
the piano held the Shakespeare pear.
Penetrating winds and big spring moons
so near earth we sicken and collapse
formed one of several segments
whose relation all this time I thought
told a story larger than what size
fool I was to stay so long in this cold room
in this drenched house of oak and ivy
where everyone has always talked in code.

The piano! The piano!
The voice inside the piano!
Her lost fingers, her secret blue sentences
inky under sheets! Her missing father! Her hand mirror!

Hold your mirror! Converge upon this flame!
The sun, dancing all alone, highlights your birthday,
the dark you share it with!
Not your fault! Not your failure!

The secret money is another form of flame,
involuntary as this poking up of rock,
this finger men have dreaded.
Crash goes the souvenir wineglass,
the fat boy in the corner can't stop crying...

The True and Secret Reason

My two hearts circle one another,
waking and sleeping, eating their bread, drinking their water,
making their tumult of puppies and babies.
Not extending, but taking other forms, their poem
hastens along, a shadow on a ceiling,
a candle responsive to the moon.

I'm an emergency case whose door a nurse left open.
I was awake, but did not stir. In the woodcut, I'm alone,
content beneath the giant moon whiting out my
bedroom window. Only you and I remain, and what the dead do
for the living is remind us what we are. I guess
it takes two hearts to face this hydra,
but acting is another word for willing,
and I am so, so willing to be your lover,
your set of keys, your window light, alert.
Even if you're not with me, our names connect
like a statue connecting with a dream about a statue
I had and would like to tell you, but not now.

I have no more idea when than the gorgeous solo moon,
cooling its head like milk poured in darkness,
going back to sleep on the carpet like a coin, far away.

Legends of the Marketplace

Lover, the hundred gulls that landed have flown off
like sleepy children. It's bright around the figure
of a puzzled clown, the spirit of the place,
dark only in some pieces of the frame. A few feet away
the clown's father mutters about money. She's his daughter
in sharp smile and ragged shoes, weeping and juggling.

Love has its plumb line in her chest too, but no one knows this.
She thinks about secrets more, goes out less
these winter days. Her winter pants, her winter blouse,
her winter with her father on the spotlit beach open
like an andropod. Their house lay built on sand
they feared and books they sold to men at night.
And oh, how good that book collection was!
Colleges agreed you could close your eyes and point,
any title you would hit would change you for the better.

Later, trees grew into heavy pieces of water. Lover,
no numbers can divide us. We came to them later than others,
who resent us for that afternoon we laughed and laughed
at their resentment. And then I had to go.

Wavering Phantom

Forget your years of toiling in a study,
intransigent instruments fitted to your hand.
Forget the upholstered strength of a piano,
how greens on a mid-March hill defined you.
After heavy rain, plants tell you what they want,
what they know you need to hear them say.
They represent life in an image of marriage.
The day crests at your feet. You find you cannot cry.
Your love-letter business suddenly stops
as though your body were ready to surrender all its habits,
and the pleading voices, gasps, dreams of being
unable to speak, unable to get up,
unable to stop the whirling above your head,
all turn luminous yellow. Your job
as caregiver for low-functioning men was ambitious
yet you carried out the plan on schedule, and
your father shook your hand over coffee and parfait.
Signs that all is full and well appear along your path.
Right away, you figure out what the dog is dreaming,
how forgiveness follows with the ooze of night. Music
really helps. Books are her subset, and your voice is
just a book: every sound you make is a brand new page.

In Distant Trees

We read our family saga through insomnia headaches,
keep hesitating in the face of its blue flame.
Spring begins at the circumference of sleep, bleeds toward one
of many centers. A folksinger performs a symphony
on a beach: it is Beethoven's Seventh, arranged for solo guitar.
A fierce wind rises against his face. At this point I realize
I will always be the son of a travelling man, flying to Pittsburgh,
Denver, Miami, a square of bright red plastic,
carefully wrapped. He calls in the middle of another dream
to tell me he wanted to tell me what I said in the middle of
a dream about a bed beneath the tiles in the bone-white kitchen
where I am always sitting on a backless chair
next to a woman with expressive hands.

These hands are another sign of spring, and
I believe her hands, I believe them again,
I forget my regret and believe my hands like
a child believing mother, and I agree again, agree,
agree with the world in spring that has started
playing Beethoven above the street of dreams.

Comical Conversations

I wrote this book in prison typing class for extra credit.
Do you see my hand, my ear, my purse, my fortress of hair
tossing in seabreeze, snoozing on deck in a pile of peanut shells?

New books arrive: twenty-four of them, sixty pages each,
funny, wise, musical, tempting as flame.
The key to this house languishes in my father's desk drawer.
Philosophical writings deepen on his bookshelf.
My resume lies before me on his desk, its misspellings
hidden only from me. The clock reads 9:25.
I am by now nearly a hour and a half late
to the single most important appointment of my adulthood.
The waltz of flowers on the sofa
pleases me more than ever now that business is
kaput, its assets folded into fabric.

The sadness out of which those books were formed
resembles a gigantic Mayan carving.
In its ugly shadow, Mayans labor, thinking revenge.
"We ought to pay attention to Mayan civilization.
It mirrors our own so tragically," wrote my father.
"Their larger-than-life-sized right eye peers out at who we are:
one part surprise, one part ritual, one part distraction.
They celebrate small mysteries in March, great ones in September.
There's still a lot left of the piano.
How much do you think you can take?"

Good Neighbors

Never forget how your wife bathes off odors of skating rinks,
paper dolls, Girl Scout cookies, lilac toilet water, your desk.

Not that notes to yourself don't help.
It's the watch face, how it waits before teasing you back.

When you sleep, your bed is you both, pillows, sheets, blankets, women,
men, sounds of distant rivers, birds shaped like shoes.

Your dream's real subject, how awkward we feel in nature, how
frightened, how repelled, washes its tiny hands in vodka.

Finished disturbing our sleep, it retires to its cabinet
on a bookshelf crowded with identical cabinets, and feels content.

Earthlings lay down their arms, their telephones.
Angels bake our bread and give us what we want, as usual.

Nine hours earlier, a mountain rose out of the sea,
city on top, suburbs below, each citizen wearing one primary color.

He doodles mirror-writing on the backs of his hands:
LOVE/HATE, LIVE/EVIL, DUST/DUST.

His wife seems to float several feet above ground, inspecting
geography and contours. Half aloud, she says "Turn right."

They have nothing interesting to say
yet their conversation creates momentum:

beautiful audiophile records of it exist,
with the stove and every light still on.

His ice will turn to blessing steam and cleansing drinks at sundown,
tappings at the window sounding more like hands than rain.

Personal Problems

My friends grow thin, break like wafers, collapse like arches of snow.
Susan tells me she has no time to make her own secrets,
Paul has flashes of such terror he cannot leave his house to buy food.
Amy, at nineteen, is weary of men and books and rituals,
while David, fifty-two, warms his room with regretful sighs.
Alison's so worried—it looks like she might lose her chance for a house.

Tom's so broke he can't ever see living in a house
that isn't his parents', who live in Maine under many feet of snow.
When Kenneth thinks of his best friend's death last year, he sighs,
but as a man, he must shed his tears in secret.
When no one's looking he carries out simple mourning rituals:
listening to "My Favorite Things," preparing Mexican food.

Sandra's officemates drive her nuts when they insist on eating junk food
in front of her, and then leave trash around. What do their houses
look like, she wonders, thinking resentfully of this awful ritual
she has to endure each noon. Fred's retired, so shoveling snow
from his front walk exhausts him. Anne's got a secret:
she's two weeks pregnant. "We're too broke for another kid," she sighs,

sounding like Naomi, who sits in her learning disability workshop, sigh-
ing and crying because on a test she wrote "foob" instead of "food."
Donald, flying back from Prague to New York, carried a secret
in his travel bag: six months of beans in the Bronx House
of Detention. Tim's truck got stuck last week in snow.
Scott broke his leg rock-climbing, figured it was a ritual

of manhood or something, and now he performs rituals
with braces and crutches and loud, exhausted sighs.

His pain pills numb and calm him like earth beneath snow,
he's less and less interested in books, sex, food,
his promising career as a model. Marian hasn't left her house
since Sunday, she told me, and she's keeping her reason secret.

I was hurt by that conversation. We used to share our secrets
in long phone conversations that were like family rituals,
but for no apparent reason, we stopped. So my house
is now the sort of place where my wife flops down on the sofa, and sighs
"Honey, I don't feel like cooking any elaborate foods
tonight," and falls asleep. Later I stir-fry some sprouts with snow

peas and green and red peppers. I hear a throng of secrets
hissing and crackling under the food, the salty ritual
of heating and stirring. I hear their sighs throughout the house.

End of May

The sounds of earth start up a beautiful war.
All evening, miraculous freshets of rain announce how May
must end, like a novel full of blood and style.
I think today is one of mourning in little, out-of-the-way places,
and I think today the mourning will not be voiced
but will be heard among silent trees and rocks through which
we walk, hands in pockets, whistling, surprised to find each other.

We live inside our curve of life, and want
that it continue. The man I dreamed I killed,
by the end of the dream he reappeared, tall and beautifully muscled;
police applauded, and my parents spoke to me again,
words of love shaped like flowers and fruit.

I felt no shame at what I said to them that day.
A new sense of play and health filled up the lawn
in front of my church school home room.
No longer agitated, my heart no longer felt wearied
with details and fear of forgetting details,
and although I still get depressed too easily, and just as easily
fall in love, this body's doing, this heart's along.

The Riverman

You've finished panicking, brick by brick,
dime by dime, word by wounded word.
The woman on the phone, the one who felt so hurt,
is leaving you alone, is leaving you alert.
She leaves you with a sense of waking in a sliver
of blue above a bank of cirrus,
like a bird looking down at acres of food
rotting if he fails to eat.
Even the backs of your hands show signs.
The teardrop-shaped cathedral window
fails to appear this time. Important numbers
wait like drums before you.
Telling your story briefly, your lips and tongue
expel each word for good. Oh you of graceful burdens,
pink-and-blue target-hearted solitary,
a birthday candle waits in a drawer
for tiny friends who live inside your chest.
Across the weir rolls the laughter of pilgrims.
A tribe of elders stand singing evening down the sky,
wondering about the clock, wondering who to call.

The Good Curve of the Year

They tell me everything continues to go well:
digestion, water tables, our navigator's wound.
Supreme success is promised if we maintain courage, but
our ship is kindling next to a landlocked stove.
We fear what our friends may do to one another: for example,
massage-parlor gift certificates wallpaper our captain's quarters.

All winter we sat with staplers and pillboxes
waiting for the right kind of dancing.
We only made comments on what we enjoyed
to save our strength
for our weak, storied future.
The girl in our saga was named "Lamina" or "Luminea" or "Liminya."
It took us all winter, writing and rewriting
that name, to learn what it meant.

Depressed, I shrug off the dark like an itch.
The last year of childhood never seemed closer or sounded clearer;
I hurry to a window, no longer knowing what the sack I carry holds.
An unobserved black cloud obscures the sun.

Other than that, nothing's up except a sense of being lit,
a glare between the silhouette and the oval around it:
the gap is life, your part is night and stone.
There is another part
you make yourself: a ladder of pencils,
a necklace of mistakes. Ancient tales are still useful,
commentaries too.

Meanwhile a canary floats out of its cage, thunder refreshes
your summer air. Fireworks pop over bays and cornfields. My name
has never been harder to pronounce
but I find a lot of things to like
hiding on walls under stripes of shade.
The war continues under many puzzling names.

The Puzzle of the Reward

(after Joseph Cornell)

You think, This weekend we'll make no plans at all,
no paintings, no movie, no calendar.
Playing back the tape days later, you hear
a ghost voice with terrible words about your birth,
insisting you're wholly responsible
for the death of prehistoric birds.
　　　　　　　　　　　　Today you float above your thefts;
rules no longer apply to your conduct. It's midmorning,
time to reconsider this day's pain, tears folded
in notebooks you never meant to keep
along with records and pieces of poetry, dusty,
wine-ringed.
　　　　　　You need to hear about an arid land
supplying natural gas to southern region
where legends say Kando was raised and may still live.
Tablets told how badly he was swindled, what he
surrendered for a measly hundred fish.
The first tablet recorded shipments of socks and
underpants. The second tablet detailed troop movements
over mountains and plains: "We recognized their songs
and knew how to flee them..."

After defeat, Kando and Rafalpaya were forced to promise
never to say certain words or speak in certain accents,
or mention certain subjects, or talk at certain times.
The third tablet dealt with widths of circles and matters of touch.
The fourth survived only partially and may require
letters of apology. You kept thinking of allusions to Shakespeare
that turned out not to be there. You asked me:
I answered you curtly, but I was alone in the room.

A Bramble

I have brought the great ball of crystal:
who can lift it?
Can you enter the acorn of light?

Ezra Pound, *Canto CXVI*

Is it your life that keeps you moving forward,
touching only leaves and twigs as they drop?
What about the man who planted the tree,
the woman who kept it dressed and fed?
When did all that begin?

There must be a photo we could find in a weathered envelope
unless that possibility too was figured in the plans.
Fall took its cards from the table and sighed.
Your violent imperative, your airplane made of coins
melts even now in the late September heat.
Pages must be finished in a glimmer,
books be read and filed away. Then cracks
appear, then scoundrels like confetti after heroism.

A scream of men and women throng in joy: that dream again.
Yes, we had total freedom of movement,
and that robust economy may return.
Fall seems again the season of movies:
bear in mind they traffic in apathy.
I have given you a generous helping of harmony.
Thank you for your inspired critique of simony.

"Wooing and molting occur in October. The mood requires
patient study." Something's in the air, some toe or finger

prodding some road, some notebook.
Like angels near retirement, saying their prayers,
the dream begins "My wildness is a winter sun,
I seethe in cloudy weather
but just the right amount of blood
my ears can take no further"

and I cannot tell what it means except
by reference to passion. It has no gender. It is sound.
It is many. It partly gives, partly takes: we look up
at it transformed. Predictions come true.
Now we know what is open, what closed.
This child, for sale all the time now. At seasons
like this one now ending, it has no buyer but you.

In the dream I look down a flight of steps,
but I am not that man.

The New Year

is neither circle nor line, but a splash
where, more than ever, I hear men described
as their mothers' favorites.
Coming to places of fragments I say,
they're what I have,
what night leaves behind for me when it goes.
Poetry is a traffic condition, a what-next in a scented car,
a child in the next seat moving, abundantly.
Evening traffic games never were my problem

but no man ever really knows his mother.
I believed for years in her greatness
but she died unrecalled by stars
or indifferent green shoulders of mountains
protecting land from colors that one day flooded it.

How did I learn the snow-smell? How did I fly?
Before I knew floods I knew where woods lay flat,
barren of all but ice beneath branches,
black against grey sky. Four is the only allowable number.
Moving warily, a little fox crosses many roads on his way
to the woods to root beneath leaves, to scratch at bark
until nothing is left, to go back to work.

Foolish Paradise

(for Marian Galczenski)

The color of our car has changed
but its position hasn't. Leaves
scrape along the sidewalk like
shellfish along the bottom of
the sea. All morning long I've been
listening for ticking sounds
under the steady thrum of bees
and drumrolls of dark traffic.
Forty-year-old wooden chairs
painted in primary colors
float upside down over West
Los Angeles; the city's legendary
feral parrots sit waiting
atop ugly black transformers
on telephone poles over
frozen-looking residential streets.
Green and yellow flames disfigure
the eastern horizon, and are those petals
or teardrops, those thirteen shapes
filling the sky?

                    Our feelings are
equally interesting: our loving,
equally immoderate. Looking
across the room at you, I remember:
nothing is familiar. Your world
comes at me shaped like stories
with clear beginnings and middles,
vague ends. How my world comes

at you is none of my business.
Still, I wish you were here. This rain
masks an undulant amount of money
that runs from my hand, and the wet air
seems filled with lost friends and cancelled
checks. I wish you were here to help
pick up the money, soak up the water.
The level of secrecy between us
gets alarming these November
afternoons. My oracle suggests
studying the past, but that's you,
and you aren't here. And you looked so
scary the last time I hung out
with you; for instance, you said
"de omnibus est dubitandum"
instead of "see ya later."

                    In my dream
you told me you wanted two children,
a boy for day, a girl for night.
I laughed at you, since your three
grown daughters were already past
thirty. Then, shyly, we undressed,
intensely embarrassed, half-expecting
a knock, eyeing one another
like rambunctious animals,
suspicious of what we knew. We
shared the square of apple-brandy
cake, drank the bottle of ale.
My damage was whimsical and pointy.
I plastered coarse-haired hunks of onyx
on the north wall of our room, arranged them
to look like a house with a white picket fence.
I interpreted my nausea as part

of my anxiety about how you and I would
get along in that house, whether we would
settle in to the business of
our feelings, sorting them,
wrapping them, placing them in baskets.

We both desire life. Will life comply?
Not influence, but calm; not
freedom, but contentment. Man and woman
surely die, and until I do, be with me.
That's what I was trying to say
about our feelings and stuff back there.
Also, this: aside from my chair,
I have nothing to give you tonight
but my hunger.

The Lord's Subject

He makes much of fog. He forgets boundaries, leaves me
continents of time. His fog roams broken hills along the coast.
I live along my forties. I rise at five, stomach in flames,
from a dream of my mother's terrible cold smile.
Her words are my fun, my cake of blacks. He repeats them
all. I repair them this morning on the winery road.
I am a crewman, I hold a flag and wear bells. My name is Cat.
The only things protecting me from him are his orange vest
and the way he drives. He is a welcome mat above a trap door.

From where I stand, his gods are birds (dogs, I mean).
His wine lacks "finish"; in the middle of my tongue
is a nothing the size of a drachma. His cheese
is expensive and imported; it tastes like
some new meat he doesn't want to admit eating.
His music is Beethoven; it sounds like a private
late night talk a man might have with a magnet.

He picks up a piece of toast before leaving,
parts the air before him on a whim.
He remembers last week, its blue moon,
and last month, with its meteor showers,
as dogs remember the taste of buried bones.
I forgot to say the thing about vomiting.
I'm his extra credit, but just for tonight.

His new instrument proves I exist if nothing else.
I told no one about him, but he knows when I pass by.
He hears November sunlight riffing in trees.
He longs to lick and lick. He waits until my train arrives
and murders twelve random men in the station.
They pose one question each before dying. I cannot

hear his answers. He loses his bread. I found it, ate it,
shat the waste, felt hotter and tighter later. He moves, but
only in certain directions. His sweat beads up his skin
into abstract meat. I gladdened at the though of my own
destruction: oh, soon. His penis leads me to contemplation.
He will not enter his house. I am an example of what happens
under his blankets. Again, I must submit.

I am punished by and for him, then he is acquitted
by a jury of birds. He sits alone with his gleaming ears.
Murder is involved in all his feeling. On the table lies
an article by Christians who have harmed him.
He takes no notice of it. He owns no mirror.
He disobeys himself. He writes another song.
I am certain he has no notes to put in it.
His wife, like mine, no longer loves him.
Easily, he accepts this unfortunate circumstance.
I buy his sugar, but it loses shape. His application turns away.

First, he kills spring. No more roots, baby animals,
darling buds. He counted his counters,
appeared with his hatchet in ugly blue C-minor
light. His interior, black and sharp and cold: the scene of
singing. He kills Peter Pan, singing. He did New York
for fifty years. He rearranged weather: I saw
his snow, then nothing. Then a catalogue of feelings
from which he chose for me. Paging past last year,
the years before, I saw his brown prints. He tells in prints.

He pulls a long thin leaf from his mouth and hates it.
Everything depends on where I was sitting when I stood
and he shot his soft, destructive load. A table stopped
the bullet, weeping. I have his scar, knotted near the gut.
He can beat his head against a dead horse, but he can't

make him drink. His half empty glass is always fuller
on the other side of the fence that makes good neighbors.
I flicked off his ant. He's so much more of a challenge
these days. I neither fused nor occluded. I wasn't sleeping.

He speaks clearly. I wasn't living in a cloud. His face makes
a cutout. I read aloud in turbulence. My son said it was time.
He had never spoken before that moment. I cued another
classic. He knew no words but he knew when his hands
were empty. I fathered. I mean, I gathered. I gathered.
I admired Bruno Walter. He broke his first lamp. A bell
rang above my head, to prove I wasn't sleeping. He told me
inside him there spins a record that never ends. No power
on earth can stop my tears, or halt my feverish dreaming.
He shouts, waves his arms and legs. He parks me up north
upon my hurt. I planned him. He said I need more people;
all I have thus far is dogs.

I strangled laughter. There's no laughter. He strode toward
his black van, words beneath his feet. At any podium,
I speak only to him. I say, don't take this personally, but
your voice is a hateful burning. He stared back and failed.
He approaches Christmas with burglary. He opens a store with blankets
of robbery. His sky curves like bowls before grinding. I grind
and sing, grind and sing. I play Mister Passion in the Passion Play.
I get pelted with wet stuff he hurls from his secret. I depart
wearing worthless checks stapled onto his ugly thin blankets.
I stopped him and shot him and shopped him around. He reopens on
All Souls' Day. He has lives in Mexico and Norway, wives
I mean, clustering around the borders of squares.

I made the mistake of taking him seriously. He dislikes
life on planet earth variously. He drops a lead quarter
in a candy machine he owns. I encourage him not to
repeat his mistakes. I billed him as Mister Soul Provider.
His idea has to do with mourning the new century in advance,
with nausea, with buttocks spread for passive sodomy,
with shirts we've come to know like flying dreams.
His solitude is pure. His fascism is pure.

He is not the past. His attraction to epitaphs is a side issue
like the demon that just rang the door, to prove I don't need him.
I depend on him for end meat. His rump roast locates
my benefit package with a single inky finger. Thursday
I chop him again. This time he stays dead. Here he comes.

A Piece of Blood

Last year, things got so bad at home
I could starve or go to work in the mine.
Before I could go down into the mine,
I had to put on metal tipped boots,
a hard hat with special lights and earmuffs,
leather gloves, and a mining belt which had
a metal ring with a rope attached,
so I could prevent myself from
falling.

This year, I was promised work above ground.
My first job was two women talking in a car
passing through a grove of blooming sugar maples.
The afternoon sky gleamed lavender, stretching out
behind one woman asking her friend for advice.
The shape of her face, tilted in asking, formed a landscape,
her words an intermittent murmur. I must have been
in the car with them, but how did I know them?
When had I met them? Where were we going?
What did these women in the car mean? Did I know
anything about their family ties, their loves, ideas,
musical tastes? How long had it been since they left
their houses, how many miles had we ridden?

Next day I attended a funeral, then drove to the house of a friend.
We drove thirty miles to a special store, where he spent
two hundred fifty dollars on groceries: steaks, lamb, chicken,
scallops, shrimp, pasta, oranges, peaches, flour, coffee,
six bottles of Italian wine. We pushed our cart through
aisles of cereals, boulevards of electronic games.

This shopping is serious, I said, as serious as a fly
moving, and like that fly, each move is a decision.
I lost the women, but found their car,
waited by it for an hour, unhurried, unbidden.
My cloak matched the landscape. I waited
without moving, a fly in mid-air. Faintly,
a bandage appeared, over her mouth, in the west.
Did I dare remove it?

                              Now the women are driving away.
Soon I will have to return to the mine.

The Kingdom of Ends

I'm in a place where guitars are strummed by waiters, and I wait
with them for further orders. No cup catches droplets that fall
from their eyes, looking so much like tears. One waiter
puts his finger to his lips. His name is Chip. Though I know him,
and love to wait with him, my home lies on an ice-floe,
so my perceptions are distorted terribly and permanently.
This telescope, for example: I can't tell which end I'm looking through.
All I see before I drop are fallen leaves half embedded in ice.
Where is that radio that keeps repeating my name?

The story of this winter afternoon, written a century ago
by a cricket on a Canadian hearth, starts out
over a mountain, where a disastrous sky watches
its clock, waiting neither for poems nor signatures.
Off in a small magnetic room, a man sits paying jasmine-scented bills,
answering barbecue-spattered postcards from America.
He pays no attention to the atlas open on the floor beside him
so he fails to notice when a blue dot takes possession of the Canada page.

I love maps, and spend hour after hour watching them move.
The other night I had the coolest dream in months.
My truck is rolling off a map of Canada, then I go to work,
then I play ping-pong in Alaska with the songwriter
who wrote the "Untimely Mediations" theme. As I look
down at the speedboat he sits in, the lake displays
map colors, small veins of ink, smallish words signing
the land. They float up all afternoon through
red-stained leaves, stiff with cold, gentle.

Swimming Back to Land

She remembers the colors of water, the shadow
a fountain makes on a hat. I can hear her voice now:
"To me, that's not a legitimate thing—a shadow. I mean,
Christmas lights stay up all year some places, never
complaining. If I kiss the reset button, darkness spreads
only as far as I can see. I don't know how brightly
this new comet shines, but it seems to be crying out."
At the matinee, a stray remark by an actress reminded us
of the ocean. She is a brave electrician to be all made up
of water. She inhales as well as I do. She hides.
My stomach contracts: she must be returning
from the West. She must be rolling in, toward
this brittle house, this small business
of coins and wire. She must be my judge,
and I a guilty man: the cell never looked
more like truth, its floor more like an opened
letter from her, spelling feeling out in round numbers.
She started training me early for this task, early
one morning, saying "Birth makes a language
of weeping and anger, labor and no fun.
Who drinks distilled earth, leaves, peat,
who says they know these tastes? Sometimes I need
the clarity of a single note. Other times, chords
demand me. Never trust the moon or the stars."
A year I can't remember must have passed,
falling apart like wet bread in my hand.
A seamstress shuts her eyes and sees no pattern.
Her favorite student also shuts her eyes. She rides
a northbound train right now, heading toward
her place of sewing, her foot-pedaled loom.

Well May the World Go
(When I'm Far Away)

Our mountains melted without our blessing.
If we'd stayed awake longer, one lawyer opined,
and if we'd cracked the Easter mystery sometime
before Christmas, we wouldn't be kneeling, picking
black leaves off our path to the forest.
We're so distracted these days
Peter Pan came by a few hours ago, but we didn't answer.
He dropped off his newspaper, the one he writes
and prints himself, you know. This issue was two inches thick
and it was all letters to and from his girlfriend,
and as we read we wondered if it wasn't just a ploy,
like a thumb stuck out for a ride. The driver never showed
but we made him out of straw and the shell of a radio.
Later, he died.
              I need my mother again, which is the
other big problem polaroiding into the April sky, so clean
after Tuesday's rain. It's nice to be living alone here now.
Armed with jello and cookies, I face down the homeless sun
but my shirt just hangs on me, reminding me of my need.
But what does she want from me tonight? Clouds like
children's drawings loiter. They've all got guns.
They loosen their muscles and turn smudgy, ashy
over a thin band of avocado green. As a mountain turns
to wind, I turn to one hidden in a bush and ask,
Cousin, what perimeter have we reached?

The Length of an Afternoon

I.

Made of fabrics no one understands
a long curtain of familiar music blossoms outward.
You take off your clothes and are perfectly tanned.
This day will save us years of explanations, for example
the two great ships in your dream, the pair
of elderly bluesman on the pier singing
ships out onto apple-green water. I see in your face
you are smaller than your beauty,
you ride within it like those two ships' crew
heading out some place that makes no
difference to the dreamer. January nights exhausted
in our attic, under a lamp the shape
of an owl, weren't anyone's real story,
despite details and side dishes.

Morning seats itself at a piano;
black keys gleam like thoughts
about a man you kind of love.
The moment stands in its clothing,
upsetting histories of paper chains.
All names of tools are forgotten.
Lights go on under what once seemed
unimportant parts of the world.
Wouldn't you rather count the lights
than try to swallow them, with your
bouquet forgotten under your right hand?

When I awoke, the massive book had arrived,
its sandpaper pages in Spanish marbled with

dated US slang. I shut the book,
sinking with love for sounds of closing
things, closed pieces of space that sit and wait
in the dark, with me, for you.

II.

Light changes Morro Rock from a confection to a flattened rhino
and books about music, murder, God and fear lie on the couch
near the *Los Angeles Times*, Sunday, February 17. The redness of the
truck pulling up the street echoes it. Adult awareness
uses whatever tools it finds along perspective rails
separating rock from truck. Gulls and fish begin their jazz.
Which one are you? And when did the river give you up
to women who found and raised you to this place
on wet, stony earth? An organ under broken asphalt
peals and peals, but only trees collaborate. Highlighted,
Morro Rock reenters the frame after another waltz
measure. February becomes, with a few garnishes,
as easily swallowed as a pearl. The rock
stays there. We agree that it stay there,
a shrug, eloquently imaged by the sound
of air blown through elaborate brass tubes by acolytes.
We love our life together, its meaning and ordinary beauty,
although Sundays disappear like chocolate cherries
and children who only want our attention
formulate words that look like them,
words like "lost" or "bump" or "rip."
It's nothing less than the world
they're after. You know it doesn't make no sense,
you're old enough to know about understanding,
how overrated it is as a response even to a concept,
let alone to your face under salmon-colored drapes.

Your English won't stretch far enough to cup the landscape
your black truck cannot flatten into snakeskin.
Bedsheets wind around things too heavy
and too true to be said except in sleep. Every day loosens
something new, like an jiggly pony thrusting his misspelled poem
into my hand (it was all mush but the title: "Tammy Terrell"),
but because it's every day, optimism and pessimism evaporate into
tiny clouds you could put in your pocket if you wanted to.
Do you? The war-torn gods, united only by fortuitous
accidents of key and tempo, stretch to transparence
like a window you realize is slowly cooling liquid
framing Morro Rock, whose many hearts, like magnetized bells
stuck to each other in a chapel, got dropped in the estuary
by the gulls. How did that get into history when what we did
never stood a chance? Despite impeccable qualifications,
we felt replaced, freed by a series of oscillations
between anxiety and relief, epic scope under intimate lighting.
Our love, for instance, entered its most dangerous phrase
one evening as we sat involved in a grisly Western.
Folk melodies reverberating in a garage recalled the taste
of fudgesicles as we paused to place a bowl on a doorstep.
Alphorn players strolled among mines and boobytraps,
calling to each other in triads: major, minor, minor.
Plain speech became an underpainting of a river we realized
couldn't stay long. We didn't mind it loitering
along that path, pointing to a distant sea we imagined
shining under an imperfectly round moon.
We walked through the one A.M. fog step after step,
talking to ourselves about love and its embankments,
where table scraps grow wings. Praying women
knelt in readiness, muttering their caution,
their hopes for blue linen, their love of natural light.
Deaf to suggestions, we tolerated their ceaseless praying,
sat apart, refused to break. I tried to answer your awful,

intrusive questions, looked up at your big teeth.
Fourteen drawing were pinned behind you
on the eastern wall: women in prayer shawls, some seated,
some standing near broken driftwood logs, some gazing toward
a digital clock, counting off seconds of contour and rain.
Stupidly, I asked if they lived happily ever after.
The rain softened corners of the boxy, wet light like a slow
explosion of flowers. A handprinted baptism of panic formed,
brightened with winter apples and news magazines.
I knew at once what your dream meant: the blank check
printed with your face gave it away.
Posed like a married woman in your grown daughter's T-shirt,
you waited, sore and hushed, for your hair to become a page
of news. You had been eating music
off your compact discs, peeling off long silver
strips, swallowing each one like an icicle.
I insisted you couldn't be happier, even
when you owned apartments in distant cities, collected
rent, fished for keys in your tiny purse, tied and untied
your red snow-hat laces, stared at phones, plane schedules.
My collection of those things was well known once.
After I gave it to you, I picked frosting
off ceiling fans, hoping music would turn
into a prayer. Now I want to know about your motives,
what remains unseen, what terrors our bodies hold
in the closed stacks of their world-famous library.
I feel so shaky on the earth these days.
Unknowingly, I have grasped the real meaning
of the legendary Lone Ranger and Tonto:
Tonto's presence, not what he does, is the crucial thing.
He is the Ranger's power, a bird inside his mask
who cries for change. He seems about to throw a discus
past rainy areas in a diorama, and fail.
Yet that stance becomes our rhythm,

our metaphor getting along under watchful eyes,
addresses, drumrolls, Pacific mists looping around
drenched houses, dripping trees, Morro Rock
quietly rafting out to sea while we sing each other to sleep.

III.

Non-illusionistic surfaces were meant as gentle reminders
of this century's sweet-and-sour upheavals, one of which just fixed its hair in
a foggy window: I checked.
Out along the sidewalk, a moment of silence
like an abandoned cereal bowl
waits to be picked up. The soul,
a cyst toward the back of the brain, casts
an inarticulate curtain over our history of talk,
leaving our love suspended with its cousin
the waning moon. A carrier brings
his night letter from 3000 miles away.
Two mountains, one from the 1940s,
another from the 1970s, present themselves; their shoes
(both pairs) are the size of galleons.
We stay away from black.
We feel troubled by the rounded edge
of a cereal bowl, a silent night letter;
we like that we have both dried into smoke.

The 1940s remain unknown to us, despite our ache
to finish our research project on the rise and fall
of General Patton. The 1970s remain. For instance,
we spent our bicentennial three-day weekend
eating and washing, like raccoons, and when our father
telephoned Monday night, neither of us could think of

a single thing to tell him about our weekend together.
We know the names of our dead, and their nicknames.
We live now where we dreamed about for years, applauding our corners
like our favorite facial features appearing in an essay
proving we were right about the new shape of Europe,
like my hand and arm draped over your waist as we lie
sleeping, recharging our cells. I heard your voice
get childlike, hobbled, start to forget its favorite dipthongs
as you spoke. I agreed with you and still do. And so
I bring you flowers, yellow daffodils in black-and-grey-striped vases.
(The clouds above these flowers are also black and grey.)
They are exercises for piano or guitar, smooth as bathroom sinks,
invisibly joined.

This is what Sophocles could have meant by destiny:
lit-up bug shapes under our nails,
shoes the size of galleons
nudging images of our parents. They cried, "My sons!
My sons!" as though we could help it;
"Might have been, might have been,
Might have been..." You tell me
we have tasted our own blood long enough.
In the gathering afternoon, leaves outside lean up
against sleep. I thought our 1970s
were nearly identical. Clearly, I erred. I recall them
as an underworked area in a painting, a stripe left
shiny like the smog that always made us
want meat. I know we see only
fragments of a halo
so we must be surrounded by it, and what does that make us?
Imagine knowing the coast of Africa only as
unparaphrasable musculature, sent
across water with arms or smoke,

you in your corner, I in mine. Daffodils wait in both, reviewing
their first hours aware of each other.

How thin the voice of reason sounds tonight.
How tough, to confront, with forgiveness and compassion, the terrifying
singularity of my own person, let alone its reflection,
you. This corner, through which so much has passed, is not you
yet we remain in it with our being, loving only one another at last.
An hour later, tears fall, and the sadness of our corners
floods the living room, the bedroom, the kitchen
where a vase of daffodils has, earlier in the evening, begun
to lose its yellow and droop, losing petal-edges to the featureless
dark. Gone, like a room of timid people
stepping back from the 20th century, planes of yellow
hide inside shoes the size of galleons, inside silent bowls.

We will never notice them again. But consequences,
says another recollected voice, consequences. The century provides
her employees with evidence of this rot in editorials
about water and its sources, children and how badly
they turned out. Disguised as one of them, I
give talks on alchemy to a throng of attentive women.
After an hour of perfectly content silence, you said
"I am no carpenter;
nevertheless, I build. I cover a city with wooden
squares, and citizens walk festively among them,
sipping drinks, faces illuminated by the same thick
candles that burned in 1969. In this way, I save getting
lost in details of landscape or names of islands
I fell in love on, since, when I get lost in details, I snap out
into vertigo, and fall from great and awful
heights, in front of always spotless windows."
The secret slipped from its cone of silence
though some put years into research,
phoning with theories and clues. I was there to learn names
of your dead, and their nicknames.

Tiny brass husbands wait beside our bed.
A door opens on a poster angel face, full frame,
who steps without feet over shoes, mirrors, sex.

IV.

We seem to sleep indefinitely now
while driving off the edge of the earth in our pickup.
The phone in its cradle makes a vivid kiss, better than actual
intercourse. Drops of amber give coherence to necklaces
of gulamine and ironwood. As keys rest under doormats,
our hunger gets shunted under prayers for new spirits,
accompanied by tide-shifting sighs of relief at no longer having
to carry our hunger up lengthy flights of stairs.

I always find myself pulling afternoons on wagons,
knowing nothing about the futures except "it will come."
Trees gleam in the sun like nests of bells.
Oval minutes fall through perfectly shaped holes, visible
nowhere on the paper which extends forever, past
the edges of the always darkening table. And it's always
my own face I see in shop windows, writing down names
and duties. Limpid grey weather waits beneath supper.
The map clears up like a rash. Civilization
exhales. Summer lies in the hands of peevish specialists.
Hearing your alarm, I rise and began
banging two great spheres together.
Right away I get invited to a wedding
and find the perfect outfit in my closet.

At this point we realize how close
to losing everything we are. What took place
between the columns seems fragile and light

as your breath as you sleep and dream of what removed
the columns . . . *that camera, that precious film*
unspooling onto the sidewalk in the sun, oh no,
those negs proved that God exists, now they're garbage . . .

This is the cry of one sphere.

The forest loses patience.

You aren't laughing.
You're getting pissed off:
you call me "The Human Meatball."

Even so, I'm still in favor of consensual sex, real religion,
crossed-out words in poems of sand.
In a frying-pan version of your face
a sudden golden siren cries amid a fracas.
The ridgepole sags to the breaking point,
my house is in danger of collapse. What I do
tonight means everything, yet
iron ropes have bound me to my bed,
and birds outside, learning to fly, mock my struggles.
They fly to a lake above the weathered poplars,
just putting forth their last white flowers.

We deal here with humble things.
Months pass before we recognize the myth beneath
the sun behind a cloud. Down the road
a condemned man laughs crazy in his cell, snapping
his fingers, drunk on his murder.
I have been looking long at him;
I know this laughing, barking man, and how he
sits up late at night, planning itineraries,
picking smash hits, inventing the United States.

In the months we've lived together, I've come to understand
how hollow was my station-wagon childhood, how full of scent and color my
adulthood on foot. Sunlight and decay are two new enemies.
Powerless against them, we see them lifesized
yet in their proper setting, proscenium arch and all.
Just listen to that stupendous crown's low rattles,
introducing evening to the plants.

We aren't "old" in any meaningful sense
although we're, you know, "older."
Cartoons and news photos I saved in a folder
marked "Collages" have grown terribly valuable.
I remember living in little fortresses
where ovens kept bedrooms damp and warm.
Night was a man who traveled through the earth,
turning out lights one by one, block by block, like
miners fingering knee-level veins of ore.
A spring breeze animated edges of shadows,
fluffed lucid dreams. Suddenly I can't remember
what could have prompted me to enter this club,
since I have no desire to gamble and can't play cards.
Suddenly I can't remember the word for "father."

The voice at the city gate bellowed all evening
for revenge, food and drink, a chance to eat the city.
The king granted us an acre of land, wrapped in
blue foil which killed everything on it
(grass, bugs, weeds, some kittens).
We had to fit it in our one-room schoolhouse, for
we were schoolboys waiting in social studies
as the room filled with construction paper schooners
with pieces of helpful advice written on yellow sails,
green sails, red sails, white.

I never would have heard them had it not been for you.
Our roles in one another's undulated lives grew
numerous as faces of students at a lecture, waiting
with alert, expectant pens. Light falls on their faces
like tiny bells poured from a stone bowl, and keeps falling.
Hand in hand, we sit with lights ringing and bouncing
all around us, too overwhelmed to speak.

But you must understand:
I have never told the truth to anyone.
My pen skips when I try to write the word, it comes out "turth" or "thurt."
I recall the ungodly number of aliases and cover stories I've employed
in the countries and towns I've called home. If I could tell you all of them
you could be my true home, my fixed address like coordinates of a summer
constellation involving you and your reading of a noble old myth
full of inspiring images and compelling situations between man and
beast. The viewer senses dimly he's part of the show by not turning
away from this random cluster to a singer by a fire,
a girl we knew by another name in school. This recollection
fails to reach that distant smoky ocean, with its tiny yachts
and tinier sailors that keep vanishing all summer. The way I did so often.
The one you chose to marry.

All this was said beneath the portrait
concealing the wall-safe with eight hundred
thousand cash: a formidable grandmother, her
mouth a crescent moon. Black bonnet, black blouse. Beneath her hand,
a bust of Orpheus. She's looking at something scary on the carpet
behind the viewer: a cricket, or a mouse.
From the backyard, cheerful masculine sounds:
a bunch of men stand drinking around a fire, saying things.
The dominant personality emerges within minutes,
then blends back into the sharp-shadowed landscape.
A mooring in a channel, bobbing. The sky,
a shuffled deck of choirs. A dog sits in topsoil, waiting for night.

A six hundred year old man
appears in your living room, his gun suddenly in your hand.
Do not resist the impulse to shoot him through the heart. He is your father,
and needs be shot, that he may regain his strength and live another century.
This is heaven. The father crumpling, rising, crumpling, rising, crumpling.
The mind's triumph. I leave them there.
Midnight seems a question of
fireflies and thunder. I reach for a phone,
a pen; I breathe underwater in clouds
of delicious white gold air. And everything
I tried today seemed new, even the size of the dusk.

Were you a man, you would move more slowly. You would be an elegy,
closing doors gently, catching them, turning the knob,
preventing the click. In this rhythm, we confront
one another: naked, alert, about to speak and leave
ourselves below overhanging clouds that resemble
paint mountains suspended over water. Through dreams
of trees and flying shoes, a doe chases you, a red gash
deep in her forehead, her gift to you forgotten.
What soundtrack fits this recurring moment? Will we know it when we
hear the tip-off to the set-up? How shall we react? Its dark brown
burnish. Its fondness for dust. Our complicity, oh la-la-la,
unstoppable. Its conga-line of laughter. Our story.

I saw hundreds running for buses, weary in retail clothing stores,
staring out windows with phones in their hands. Their stories,
not ours. Less than one second between them. Parked in my voice like houses
on what used to be a farm. Below solid earth, rushing water.
And always the image of a troupe of clowns,
falling over themselves on the golf course they invaded.

You would put it differently:
the whole summer can be cancelled any moment
by something simple as a letter to the editor.

Scholars report they've seen lots of examples, viz.:
"The first of the poems were nothing more than placid records
of domestic events. An event makes its own music
when you are in perfect accord with it" (Nietzsche,
My Sister and I, p. 34). But proof isn't music.
It's aggression wearing gloves in warm, soapy water,
part of a blueprint, speaking as fast as humanly possible
from a cloud.

Everything we see, everything we touch,
everything on earth has its own color
and we must learn their ugly names, and use them
with each other when we speak of private things.
I was in the middle of a thought
when you walked in, exhaling loudly.
How could I explain to you how I knew about the tragedy
that was destined to start up in thirty minutes?
It's the nature of things to be apocalyptic,
to rotate crops and make dinner plans.
A lovely young woman told me her name:
Sabree Loveall. We exchanged our favorite ideas
but realized they were signs of illness, a long illness
unwinding in increments over a map of Europe
like a carpet of eucalyptus leaves. Sabree Loveall's friend
Suebob Davis lived nearby with the sisters Etna and Mehta.
Things were at a standstill, and with the phone shut off,
the only things left to live on were rumor and songs
about the past. Mothers left their sons fortunes later on,
and historians praised the phase for days, and gazed
at keys, wondering what doors they could have fit. I liked
Sabree Loveall's apartment and her neighbor Suebob Davis
but I didn't like her roomies Etna and Mehta, who refused
me, so even though they were sweet, retired old biddies
in their sixties, I had to murder them both.

Their treasure lay wasted in their ruined hands. I took it,
did much good with it. Now their names will resonate
for years, learned by heart by children, mentioned in passing
everywhere I go, on my afternoon jaunts, before supper.

Suddenly we feel certain we exist.

Thus all holes made full again, and all flat surfaces undulant.
Centuries pass and meaning changes, blue to pink like the summer evening,
able at last to stop its tears. A place in the world. Wonderful dinners.
The pregnant moon, orange, lit from within.

You're sitting beneath it with three close friends, sharing vegetable soup.
The white china tureen. My gladness at knowing I'm removed.
The chairs, so comfortably padded. Impossible to resist sleep.
The soup nourishes you in my absence. Zucchini, carrots,
cubed potato, tomato, onion in broth,
Parmesan floating on the surface like a cloud
in which I sit concealed. Music thumps and shifts around your heads.
Do we deserve this blessing? The book got written,
waitresses removed dirty plates in perfect order.
The afternoon curled around an obelisk of impressionist music, like a cat,
and won us. We were the ones who got away, the ones the afternoon
couldn't keep, despite its seductive chaos and scent of amaryllis. That soft song
we hear is its lament for us. No, it's just the radio breeze of a passing car.
It's always 1968 in the chassis.

Then the children in the playground fell silent.
A helicopter chattered overhead.
Was it going to drop toys or candy or coupons for the circus?
One nine-year-old connoisseur of horror flicks
felt her face grow warm with the thought that giant grasshoppers
or serial murderers would parachute down and devour her in

video carnage. Her parents decided at that moment not to drive
to Los Angeles after all, but to celebrate her birthday at their home.
Her mother remembered the birth, the doctor's sharp voice, the Indian
flute raga tape governing her breath. By then the helicopter was long gone,
leaving only the afternoon hum, the creak of the seesaw and swings.

About the Author

JAMES CUSHING was born in Palo Alto in 1953 and attended the Harvard School and the University of California, where he studied poetry with George Hitchcock and John Ashbery and earned his Ph.D. In the early eighties, he hosted a live poetry radio program on KPFK-FM in Los Angeles and directed the Al's Bar Poetry Series. His previous collection of poetry, *You and the Night and the Music* (1991), was also published by the Cahuenga Press of Los Angeles. The 1994 winner of *Renegade* magazine's "Warlord of the Subculture" award, Cushing teaches on the English faculties of California Polytechnic State University and Cuesta College, both in San Luis Obispo. He hosts jazz on radio station KCPR-FM and performs on voice, guitar and keyboards with his experimental jazz-rock-poetry unit, The Jimm Cushing Paradox.

Of the poems in *The Length of an Afternoon*, Cushing writes: "In my previous book, I was working off the notion that jazz standards were imaginary places where complex feelings are assigned clearly articulated thematic centers which I could then vary to suit my own experience. The first poem here, 'Our Love Is Here to Stay,' marked the completion of that work. Since then, I've been bundling up what I learned in those imaginary places, and allowing thematic centers to grow out of the bundle. Most of the poems in this book concern the way human time astonishes with its continual simultaneous creation and dismantling of meaning, cycling its children through dreaming and waking, dancing and sitting still, living in intimacy and living in solitude, acting in history and in one's imagination, being borne from the water to the shore and back: 'activity, not communication' (John Cage)."